Discover & Learn

Vikings

Years 5-6

This book is for pupils studying KS2 History
in Years 5 and 6 (ages 9-11).

It's full of facts, sources and questions covering
'The Viking and Anglo-Saxon struggle for the Kingdom of
England to the time of Edward the Confessor'
— perfect for exploring and understanding the whole topic.

3 0116 02040330 7

Picture acknowledgements

Cover photo © Look and Learn.

p2 - p9

p2 (Viking ship) Private Collection / Bridgeman Images. p4 (background runes) © The Art Archive / Alamy. p4 (runestone) © PhotoAlto sas / Alamy. p5 (Holy Island of Lindisfarne) © iStockphoto.com/stephensavage. p5 (Lindisfarne Priory) © iStockphoto.com/gannett77. p6 (rainbow) © iStockphoto.com/Henrik_L. p7 (Thor) © iStockphoto.com/Grafissimo. p7 (Valhalla) © Ivy Close Images / Alamy. p8 (coins) © Heritage Image Partnership Ltd / Alamy. p9 (L'Anse aux Meadows) De Agostini Picture Library / C. Sappa / Bridgeman Images. p9 (Viking ship) © iStockphoto.com/rimglow.

p10 - p19

p10 (longship) Mark Harris/Photolibrary/Getty Images. p11 (slave market) © National Geographic Image Collection / Alamy. p11 (scales) © Heritage Image Partnership Ltd / Alamy. p12 (Lindisfarne Priory) Private Collection / © English Heritage Photo Library / Bridgeman Images. p13 (monastery raid) National Geographic Creative / Bridgeman Images. p14 (Viking sword) © Hull and East Riding Museum, Humberside, UK / Bridgeman Images. p15 (Thingvellir) © iStockphoto.com/TimothyBall. p15 (Law Rock) © iStockphoto.com/tupungato. p16 (Tynemouth) National Trust Photographic Library/Derrick E. Witty / Bridgeman Images. p16 (Orkney) © SJ Images / Alamy. p17 (coast) © Mary Evans Picture Library. p17 (tin) Dorling Kindersley/UIG/SCIENCE PHOTO LIBRARY. p18 (Ragnar) © Look and Learn.

p20 - p29

p21 (paying the Vikings) © Look and Learn. p21 (London coins) © York Coins Inc. p21 (King Alfred) © Guildhall Art Gallery, City of London / Bridgeman Images. p22 (Somerset) © Adam Burton/Robert Harding World Imagery/Getty Images. p22 (Guthrum baptism) © iStockphoto.com/duncan1890. p23 (Alfred's ships) © Look and Learn. p23 (Alfred the Great) © iStockphoto.com/ZU_09. p24 (Aethelfleda) © Mary Evans Picture Library. p25 (brooche image from The Anglo-Saxon Laboratory, http://www.aslab.co.uk/ © Northern Archaeological Associates. p26 (archaeologist) Ancient Art and Architecture Collection Ltd. / Bridgeman Images. p26 (Viking boot) © Ancient Art & Architecture Collection Ltd / Alamy. p27 (wooden cups and bowls) © York Archaeological Trust. p27 (comb and case) © The Trustees of the British Museum. p28 (King Athelstan) © Mary Evans Picture Library. p29 (Dunnottar) © iStockphoto.com/Canonite. p29 (Battle of Brunanburh) Private Collection / The Stapleton Collection / Bridgeman Images.

p30 - p39

p30 (Rollo) © David Robertson / Alamy. p31 (runestone) © Mary Evans/Interfoto Agentur. p31 (Olaf) © Clement Guillaume / Bridgeman Images. p32 (shore raid) © North Wind Picture Archives / Alamy. p33 (Danegeld) Private Collection / Bridgeman Images. p34 (Canute stained glass) Canterbury Cathedral, Kent, UK / Sonia Halliday Photographs / Bridgeman Images. p35 (Queen Emma) © British Library Board. All Rights Reserved / Bridgeman Images. p36 (King Edward) © Neil Holmes / Bridgeman Images. p37 (tapestry) © Image Asset Management Ltd. / Alamy. p38 (seal) © Montagu Images / Alamy. p38 (court) © Lambeth Palace Library, London, UK / Bridgeman Images. p39 (tapestry) Musee de la Tapisserie, Bayeux, France / With special authorisation of the city of Bayeux / Bridgeman Images.

Contents

Published by CGP

Written by Joanna Copley

Editors: Katherine Faudemer, Hayley Thompson

Reviewer: Alison Griffin

ISBN: 978 1 78294 201 6

With thanks to Rachel Kordan and Sophie Scott for the proofreading.

With thanks to Laura Jakubowski for the copyright research.

Every effort has been made to locate copyright holders and obtain permission to reproduce sources. For those sources where it has been difficult to trace the originator of the work, we would be grateful for information. If any copyright holder would like us to make an amendment to the acknowledgements, please notify us and we will gladly update the book at the next reprint. Thank you.

Printed by Elanders Ltd, Newcastle upon Tyne

Clipart from Corel®

Who Were The Vikings?

Timeline

	Vikings first raid England	VIKINGS IN ENGLAND	Final Viking attack on England
AD 600	AD 800	AD 1000	AD 1200 Today

The Vikings came from the lands we now call Norway, Sweden and Denmark. This area is called Scandinavia. The Vikings were 'Norsemen'.

What do you think Norsemen means?

Norsemen means the men of the North.

The men who came by boat

<u>Fame</u> and <u>wealth</u> were very important to the Norsemen. They could get both by <u>raiding other lands</u>. Norsemen who travelled abroad by <u>sea</u> on raids were called <u>Vikings</u>.

The Vikings were exploring and raiding from the end of the 8th century until the middle of the 11th century. They travelled across the seas in ships called longships.

What do you think it would have been like to travel on a Viking ship?

The sea pirates are coming

The first Viking raids to Britain, from about AD 790 to 850, were <u>short trips</u> to <u>steal treasure</u> and <u>take slaves</u>. These early raids only happened every so often, and only a few ships came each time.

This map shows some <u>routes</u> that Vikings took on their way to Britain and Ireland.

Later on, Vikings <u>settled</u> in Britain.

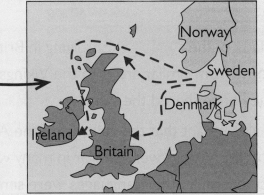

> *Can you think of any reasons why the Vikings might have wanted to settle in Britain?*

Historians think it was because Britain had a <u>warmer climate</u> than where they had come from, and also had <u>fertile land</u> — perfect for growing crops.

From farming to fighting

To own a ship and get it ready for raiding, a Norseman would have to have some money. They would probably be <u>landowners</u>, with <u>wives</u> who could run their farm while the Vikings were away raiding, and enough <u>slaves</u> to leave working on the farm. The <u>crew</u> of the Viking ship would be <u>younger men</u>, hoping to make <u>money</u> and <u>a name</u> for themselves.

The men would raid in between farming — a landowner might oversee the planting of crops in the spring, raid until harvest time, make sure the harvest was safely in, and then go back to raiding until the winter storms made the seas unsafe.

> *Which do you think the Norsemen preferred doing — farming or raiding? Why?*

> *If you were a Viking, which one would you have preferred to do?*

Stealing gold and silver by force

The Vikings explored further than anyone who had come before them, killing and stealing as they went. They sound like a bit of a rough bunch! Now you know who they were, it's time to look at how the Vikings were different to the Anglo-Saxons.

Viking Values

Many of the Anglo-Saxons living in Britain had originally come from similar areas to the Vikings. This meant that they once shared the same Pagan religions.

It also meant that the cultures of the Anglo-Saxons and the Vikings were similar in many ways. For example, their languages were similar.

> Many Pagan religions worship several gods and goddesses, and nature is seen as being very important.

This Viking poem has been written out in Old English, which the Anglo-Saxons spoke, and Old Icelandic, which some Vikings spoke.

What similarities can you spot between the two languages?

Old English:

"Þæt mælede mín módor
þæt me scolde ceapian
flæge and fægra ára,
faran aweg wið wícingum
standan úppe in stefnan,
stíeran deorne cnear,
faran swá tó hæfene,
héawan man and óðer.

Old Icelandic:

"Þat mælti mín móðir,
at mér skyldi kaupa
fley ok fagrar árar,
fara á brott með víkingum
standa upp í stafni,
stýra dýrum knerri,
halda svá til hafnar
höggva mann ok annan.

Writing on runestones

Runestones are standing stones engraved with runes — the alphabet used by the Vikings. They sometimes have pictures too. The Vikings wrote tributes to friends, family and their gods on runestones, as well as tales of voyages to other lands.

Clashing with Christianity

When the Vikings began to raid Britain, they followed a Pagan religion. By then though, the Anglo-Saxons in Britain had become Christians. Peaceful monasteries and priories had been built — places where <u>monks</u> lived and worshipped. Many of these were <u>raided</u> by Vikings.

These pictures show the island of Lindisfarne and the remains of a priory there. The original priory on the island was raided by Vikings in AD 793.

> Lindisfarne was an easy target for the Vikings.
> Why do you think this was?

The monks lived quiet, peaceful lives, studying the teachings of <u>Christ</u>. It's easy to imagine how they felt when a load of screaming Viking warriors turned up!

How to be a Viking

The <u>Havamal</u> is a poem that was written to advise Vikings on <u>how to behave</u>.
It praises good manners, honour, truth and bravery. Below is an extract from the Havamal.
It gives advice about how to behave in battle:

An eleventh I know, I if needs I must lead
To the fight my long-loved friends;
I sing in the shields, I and in strength they go
Whole to the field of fight,
Whole from the field of fight,
And whole they come thence home.

> How are Viking warriors supposed to behave in battle according to this part of the poem?

> Why was this behaviour important?

Runestones can tell us a lot about the Vikings

The words that are engraved on to runestones can tell us a lot, because they were written by the Vikings themselves. Runestones have been known to celebrate the lives of Vikings killed on raids, and to describe expeditions across the seas.

Norse Beliefs

Timeline

Vikings first raid England

Vikings raid Lindisfarne

Final Viking attack on England

AD 600   AD 800   AD 1000   AD 1200   Today

Norse religion provides a clue to why Vikings valued bravery and a 'good death' in battle.

Can you think of any reasons why having a 'good death' in battle might have been important to the Vikings?

How <u>brave</u> you had been in death decided where you went in the afterlife.

In a different world

The Norsemen believed that the world was actually a set of nine worlds.

These were called:

<u>Midgard</u>, the only place where humans lived,

<u>Asgard</u>, the home of the Aesir gods and goddesses,

<u>Vanaheim</u>, the home of the Vanir gods and goddesses,

<u>Jotunheim</u>, the home of the giants,

<u>Niflheim</u>, a world of ice,

<u>Muspelheim</u>, a world of fire,

<u>Alfheim</u>, the home of the elves,

<u>Svartalfheim</u>, the home of the dwarves,

<u>Helheim</u>, the home of the goddess Hel and the kingdom of the dead.

Can you think of how rainbows might be tied in with Norse beliefs about the nine worlds?

The Norsemen believed that a rainbow <u>bridge</u> called <u>Bifrost</u> joined Midgard with Asgard.

Lots of gods to choose from

There were many Norse gods. Here are a few:

1. The father of the gods was called <u>Odin</u>.
2. Odin's wife was called <u>Frigg</u>.
   She was the goddess of love.
3. <u>Thor</u> was the god of thunder,
   and protected humans.
4. <u>Tyr</u> was the god of war and justice.

The Norsemen told many stories about their gods. These stories often involved mythical creatures like giants and elves. We still tell stories about Norse gods today.

Have you heard of any stories involving Norse gods?

Why do you think stories are still told about these gods?

The afterlife – time to party?

Vikings believed that if they died fighting bravely, they would be taken from the battlefield to Valhalla, a hall in <u>Asgard</u>, where <u>Odin</u> ruled.

These Vikings would become <u>heroes</u> in the afterlife. Each day they feasted and drank in Valhalla — where the mead never ran out.

Norsemen that didn't die bravely in battle went to <u>Helheim</u> when they died. In one part of Helheim, evil and dishonest people were <u>punished</u>. However, there were also areas of Helheim for <u>good people</u> who weren't warriors.

Judgement by the gods...

With the choice of either Valhalla or Helheim before them, it is easy to see why Viking warriors appeared to have no fear of death in battle — it was preferable to die honourably, rather than of old age or sickness, as the afterlife was so much better!

Viking Voyages

Timeline

| | Vikings first raid England | Vikings raid Lindisfarne | | Vikings settle in Newfoundland | Final Viking attack on England | | | |

AD 600   AD 800   AD 1000   AD 1200   Today

The Vikings believed that dying <u>honourably in battle</u> lead to an afterlife as a <u>hero</u>.

Why might this belief have had an influence on the Viking raids?

Hoards of silver and gold

We can tell where the Vikings visited from archaeological evidence. It seems that they travelled very widely — there is evidence that they travelled to England, Scotland, Ireland, Northern and Central Europe, and Russia.

What sort of evidence do you think archaeologists might have found to show that the Vikings travelled to other countries?

Archaeologists have found items in Viking hoards that have come from distant lands — this is good evidence that the Vikings travelled to other countries.

For example, a hoard of <u>coins</u> was found in Sweden in 2008 which was buried in around AD 850. A lot of these coins originally came from <u>Arabic</u> countries such as Syria and Iraq, so it's likely that the Vikings travelled there.

A hoard of silver items found in the Furness area of England in 2011 also contained some <u>Arabic coins</u>.

Many Viking hoards of coins or precious metals contain objects from the coasts of southern Europe.

West to Canada?

You might think that it wasn't possible for the Vikings to travel as far west as Canada — it's a long way from where they came from. However, sagas record that people did. Leif Ericsson is supposed to have travelled that far.

Remains of a Viking settlement have been found at a site in Newfoundland in Canada called l'Anse aux Meadows. The site has now been rebuilt.

The remains at the site show that Vikings did sail all that way and settle. It also seems that they traded up and down the coast.

Viking objects such as pins, knitting needles and spindles were found at the settlement.

Who do you think would have used objects like these?

Do you think these objects provide evidence that Viking women travelled to Canada too?

No hopping on a plane for the Vikings

The Vikings would have sailed across the seas in ships like the one below.

Do you think the journey would have been difficult in a ship like this? Why, or why not?

How do you think the Vikings found their way across the sea?

The Vikings didn't have satellite navigation or even compasses. They would use the Sun and stars to navigate. When they were in sight of the shore, they would look out for landmarks to guide them.

Pretty well-travelled folks...

It's impressive that the Vikings made it to places so far away. Remember, back then, boats didn't have engines! We can tell a lot about where the Vikings travelled by the things that archaeologists find — some items come from a long way outside Scandinavia.

Raiding and Trading

Timeline

| AD 600 | Vikings first raid England | VIKINGS IN ENGLAND | Final Viking attack on England | AD 1200 | Today |

AD 600   AD 800   AD 1000   AD 1200   Today

The Vikings were very successful <u>raiders</u> and <u>traders</u>.

Can you think of any reasons why the Vikings were so successful?

The Vikings' secret weapon

Vikings loved the sea, and they were <u>master sailors</u>. This gave them the opportunity to travel far and wide. The Vikings had two main types of <u>ship</u>:

1. The knarr, which was sturdy and strong for moving cargo and animals.
2. The longship, which was fast, light and easy to move for raiding.

Viking boats were <u>flexible</u>, which meant they could bounce about on the waves in storms. They were made of curved, overlapping wooden planks, joined together with iron fastenings. These planks were so <u>strong</u> that the sides of the boat only needed to be 2-3 cm thick.

The picture below shows a Viking longship kept in a museum in Norway.

What features do you think this longship has that might make it good in a raid?

The structure of the boat means it can be sailed in <u>shallow water</u> right up to the beach. Also, because it's <u>double-ended</u>, it can be quickly pushed off the beach again <u>backwards</u>, and rowed away to sea.

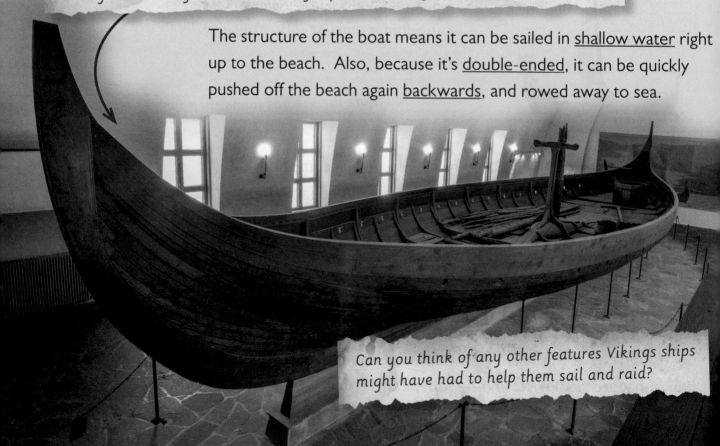

Can you think of any other features Vikings ships might have had to help them sail and raid?

Raiding, trading and slaving

The Vikings traded products from Scandinavia (such as amber, ivory, and <u>animal furs</u>) with countries <u>overseas</u>.

They also traded in <u>slaves</u>. Slavery had been accepted throughout Europe and Asia for centuries. The Vikings captured slaves on their raids into other countries and would sell them in <u>markets</u> abroad. This picture gives an artist's idea of what a slave market might have looked like.

Vikings also took slaves home for their <u>own use</u>.

What do you think the Vikings needed slaves for?

Goods for sale

The Vikings <u>stole</u> items that were of value to them on <u>raids</u>. But they also traded with people for items on trips abroad. In exchange for the goods they traded, the Vikings received things like <u>silver</u>, <u>gold</u>, <u>silk</u>, <u>glass</u> and <u>fine pottery</u>.

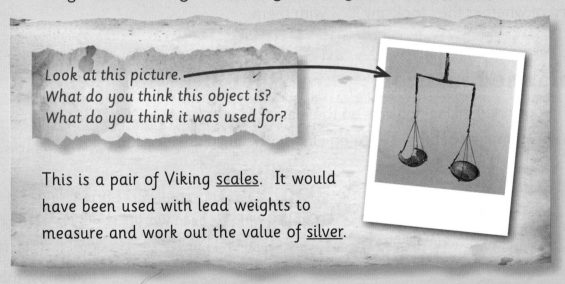

Look at this picture.
What do you think this object is?
What do you think it was used for?

This is a pair of Viking <u>scales</u>. It would have been used with lead weights to measure and work out the value of <u>silver</u>.

Ships and the sea were vital for a Viking's business

Travelling by sea wouldn't have been easy, but the design of their ships probably helped a lot. Sea travel was vital for the Vikings to be able to <u>trade</u>. Once in other countries, they would take what they wanted, or trade the things they'd brought with them.

Viking Visits

Timeline

Vikings first raid England	Vikings raid Lindisfarne	Final Viking attack on England	

AD 600   AD 800   AD 1000   AD 1200   Today

This map shows what Europe looks like today. Some modern countries are labelled. The countries the Vikings came from are coloured orange.

> From the map, can you suggest why the Vikings came to Britain on their early raids?

> If you were a Viking, where would you have gone on your raids?

First voyage to England

The first known Viking visit to Britain was in about <u>AD 787</u>. The Vikings sailed to Britain and landed at Portland on the south coast. The local tax official mistook them for traders, and tried to make them pay taxes. The Vikings killed him, and sailed away. There's no record of whether they took any loot with them.

A planned mission

The first planned Viking <u>raid</u> was on the island of Lindisfarne, in <u>AD 793</u>. A small community of <u>monks</u> lived on Lindisfarne in an undefended priory.

> What do you think Lindisfarne priory had that would have been worth stealing?

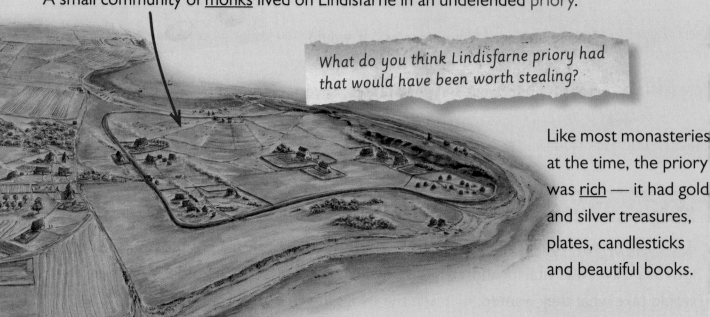

Like most monasteries at the time, the priory was <u>rich</u> — it had gold and silver treasures, plates, candlesticks and beautiful books.

Time to make some cash

Over the next few years, the Vikings <u>rampaged</u> around the country, fighting anyone who got in their way. One tactic appears to have been to <u>fight</u> a battle, agree to be <u>paid</u> to go away, and then to <u>move on</u> to the next place!

These coins are from a hoard found in London.

The hoard dates back to AD 871-872. It's thought to have been <u>buried</u> by an Anglo-Saxon living there at the time of a <u>Viking attack</u>.

Why do you think the person who owned these coins might have buried them?

How do you think this person might have felt about the Viking attacks?

Victory at last?

In AD 871, <u>Alfred</u> became king of Wessex and made peace with the Vikings. Alfred managed to <u>pay off</u> the Vikings and keep the peace for <u>five whole years</u> — but in AD 876 a new leader of the <u>Danish Vikings</u> attacked Wessex. This new leader was called <u>Guthrum</u>.

Alfred fought against Guthrum for two years, but in early 878, the Vikings attacked Alfred at Chippenham and killed many of his men. Alfred ran away to Somerset and it seemed as if the <u>last Anglo-Saxon king</u> had been <u>defeated</u>.

Do you think Alfred was right to give the Vikings money? Do you think he thought the peace he bought would last?

The Vikings drove a hard bargain...

...and often went back on their word. By 878, only one man stood between them and controlling all of England: Alfred, King of Wessex. Alfred would later become known as Alfred the Great. Let's turn over and find out more about him...

Alfred the Great

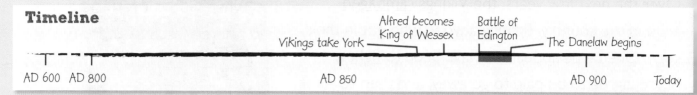

Timeline

Vikings take York — Alfred becomes King of Wessex — Battle of Edington — The Danelaw begins

AD 600 AD 800   AD 850   AD 900   Today

In 878, the Anglo-Saxons were on their knees. All the kingdoms except Wessex had either been defeated, or had given in and paid the Vikings for peace. Alfred, King of Wessex, was in hiding in the Somerset marshes. This picture shows the place Alfred was hiding.

Can you think why Alfred might have chosen this as a place to hide out?

So why is Alfred known as Alfred the Great?

You can't keep a great man down

Alfred didn't stay defeated for very long. After a short time in the marshes, he raised an army and beat the Danish Vikings at the <u>Battle of Edington</u> in May 878.

Alfred and <u>Guthrum</u>, the leader of the Danes, made a treaty. As part of the treaty, Guthrum had to be baptised as a <u>Christian</u>. Guthrum then had to <u>leave Wessex</u> and retreat to East Anglia. England was <u>safe</u> from Viking raids — for a while.

This is a picture of Guthrum being baptised.

Why do you think Alfred might have wanted the Viking Guthrum to become a Christian?

The Vikings had proved themselves untrustworthy. Maybe Alfred hoped that being a Christian would make Guthrum keep his promises. He was wrong!

The Vikings go back on their word... again

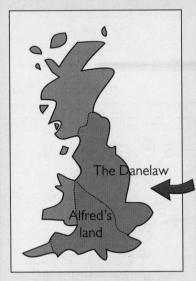

Peace lasted in Wessex until 884, when Guthrum attacked again, but was defeated by Alfred. Alfred forced Guthrum to sign another treaty.

Mercia was split, with Alfred taking the south and west, and the Danish Vikings taking the east and the north.

The Danes now owned an area of Britain, which they ruled from York. This area was called the Danelaw.

The Danelaw

Alfred's land

Alfred ended up giving a large area of land to the Vikings even though he beat them. Why do you think he did this?

Alfred really was great...

Alfred re-organised the army, and changed battle methods so that it was easier to fight the Vikings. He built longships to fight the Vikings at sea and he won many sea-battles against them.

...and not just in battle

Alfred valued learning. Education in England at the time was very poor because of the Viking attacks.

How do you think the Viking attacks might have affected education in England?

Viking attacks destroyed the monasteries where people were taught. To help, Alfred had books translated from Latin, which he sent to the bishops, so they could use them to teach.

He also set up his own school and he ordered the Anglo-Saxon Chronicle to be written about the history of the Anglo-Saxons.

Alfred – a king deserving of his nickname?

Alfred did a lot of great things to help England. He defeated the Vikings in several battles and managed to keep part of England under Anglo-Saxon control. He also did a lot to help the English people themselves — especially in terms of education.

The Danes and the Danelaw

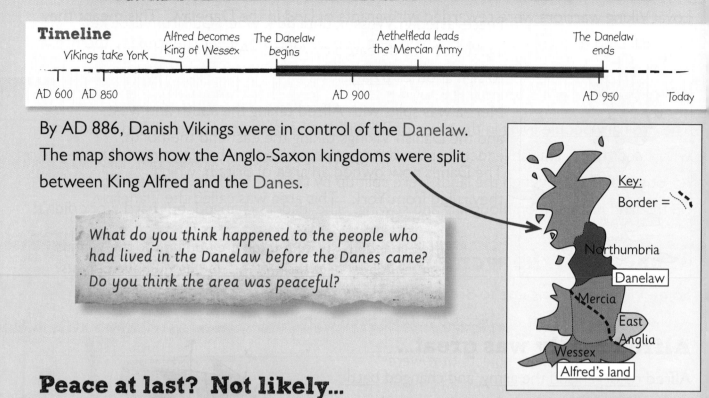

Timeline

Vikings take York — Alfred becomes King of Wessex — The Danelaw begins — Aethelfleda leads the Mercian Army — The Danelaw ends

AD 600 AD 850 — AD 900 — AD 950 — Today

By AD 886, Danish Vikings were in control of the Danelaw. The map shows how the Anglo-Saxon kingdoms were split between King Alfred and the Danes.

> What do you think happened to the people who had lived in the Danelaw before the Danes came? Do you think the area was peaceful?

Key:
Border =

Northumbria

Danelaw

Mercia

East Anglia

Wessex

Alfred's land

Peace at last? Not likely...

Even after the Danelaw was made, fighting went on between the Anglo-Saxons and the Danes for many years. Both sides made raids across the border. Anglo-Saxon Mercia, which bordered the Danelaw, was not a peaceful place to be.

Defence against the Danes

King Alfred's eldest daughter, Aethelfleda, helped to defend Anglo-Saxon land from the Danes. She was married to the leader of Anglo-Saxon Mercia, Aethelred. After her husband became ill, Aethelfleda led the Mercian army. Aethelfleda kept the Danes out of English Mercia, and after her husband died in AD 911, she took charge of its defence. Aethelfleda fortified Mercian towns against the Danes and built many fortresses.

This is an artist's impression of Aethelfleda leading the Mercian army.

> How do you think the Vikings might have reacted to seeing a woman leading an army? Why do you think this?

Dishing out the Danelaw

Loyal Viking warriors were rewarded with grants of land in the Danelaw. This meant they were allowed to throw out Anglo-Saxon landowners, and take over the land for themselves.

Working for a new leader

The ordinary people living in the areas of Britain that became the Danelaw had no say in who ruled them. Danish leaders replaced Anglo-Saxon leaders, but farming had to go on, or no-one would eat. When the lands were split up by the war leaders, people who worked on the land just went on ploughing and sowing. The leaders changed, but hard work didn't!

What about the women?

Some Viking women came to Britain to settle in the Danelaw. We know this because of objects that have been found in graves.

Here are some objects that were found in a Viking grave in Yorkshire.

What do you think they are?*

Many Vikings would have settled down and taken a wife from among the Anglo-Saxon women. As soon as Vikings started settling down, the people began to mix.

Life would have been hard for a woman whose male relations had died, as she would have had difficulty supporting herself. She would have had to live and work with her conquerors or starve.

How do you think these Anglo-Saxon women might have felt about marrying Vikings?

Time for some new leaders...

Life around the border between the Danelaw and England probably wouldn't have been very calm, as there was a lot of fighting over who owned the land. For ordinary people though, life went on. Wessex and Northumbria would have been quieter places to be!

*These are a Viking woman's brooches.

Viking Jorvik

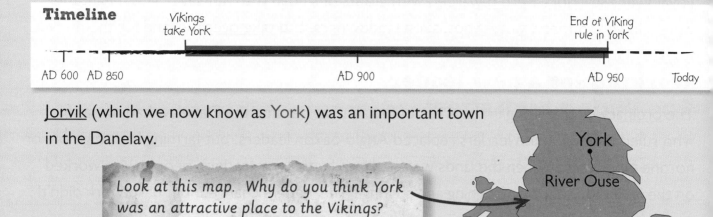

Vikings take York   End of Viking rule in York

AD 600   AD 850   AD 900   AD 950   Today

Jorvik (which we now know as York) was an important town in the Danelaw.

Look at this map. Why do you think York was an attractive place to the Vikings?

York

River Ouse

Making York home

York was probably very attractive to the Vikings because from the coast they could <u>sail</u> right up the <u>River Ouse</u> to the town. This <u>link to the sea</u> also meant they could easily <u>trade</u> with countries overseas.

Most Viking settlement in York was in an area that sits between two rivers. This would have been <u>easy to defend</u> as the rivers would have formed a natural boundary.

River Foss

Viking Jorvik

River Ouse

Digging for clues

We know a lot about Viking settlement in York from excavations in an area called <u>Coppergate</u>. These excavations have helped to show how Vikings lived in York.

The earth around Coppergate is <u>soft</u> and <u>wet</u>. This stopped many items buried there from rotting away. It also meant archaeologists were able to dig down a long way. They found remains of a huge range of things, from <u>pottery</u> to <u>clothing</u>.

This is a Viking leather boot excavated in Coppergate in York.

WALL OF HOUSE C

What does this tell us about Viking clothing?

Life in the city

Jorvik was laid out in a <u>grid</u> pattern, with little streets lined with houses built of <u>wood</u>. There were <u>shops</u> and <u>workshops</u>, <u>toilets</u>, <u>animals pens</u> and <u>wells</u> in between the houses. People lived close together in a smelly, noisy, dirty environment.

The Viking high street

Viking York was a place with links to the wider world.
For example, archaeologists found a cap made with silk from Turkey.
They've also found a shell from the Red Sea and pottery wine jars from Germany.

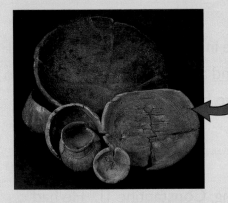

Along with evidence of trade, there is evidence of <u>craft</u> and <u>industry</u>. 'Coppergate' actually means 'street of the cup-makers' and there are workshops that produced <u>wooden cups and bowls</u>. We know other small workshops made <u>leather</u>, <u>shoes</u> and <u>boots</u>, from finding off-cuts of leather there.

Metals were brought from other places in Britain or Europe, and turned into pins, brooches, rings, knives and small hand tools. There was also a workshop which made items in <u>bone</u> and <u>antler</u>.

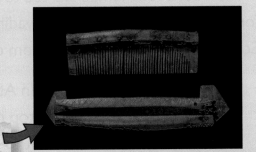

Can you tell what this is?

This is a comb and comb case made of bone. It was excavated in Coppergate.

What's for dinner...?

The Coppergate excavations also provided evidence of what people <u>ate</u>.

What sort of things do you think were found?

Large amounts of <u>pig</u>, <u>cow</u> and <u>sheep</u> bones have been discovered. Archaeologists can also tell that the Vikings ate <u>wheat</u> and <u>barley bread</u>, many different <u>plants</u>, and flavoured their food with <u>celery</u> and <u>herbs</u>. They also had <u>fish</u>, <u>oysters</u> and <u>fruits</u>.

How does it compare to life today?

The Anglo-Saxons and the Vikings were around hundreds of years ago, but archaeologists can find things that tell us a lot about what life would have been like for them. Very clever.

Athelstan and Constantine

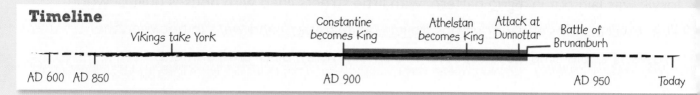

Remember Alfred the Great? He had a grandson called <u>Athelstan</u>, who played a big part in the history of England.

What can you remember about Alfred the Great and his family?

Alfred the Great's grandson, Athelstan, came to the throne in AD 925. Athelstan turned out to be a powerful and successful king, who <u>united England</u> as one kingdom and tried to unite <u>Britain</u>. But how did this happen? First, we need to go back to AD 900...

Introducing Constantine

In AD 900, Scotland had started to unite under a strong king, <u>Constantine II</u>. He had forced the Vikings who were invading Scotland to retreat, and by 904 was re-organising the Scottish tribes into a new kingdom called <u>Alba</u>.

In AD 918, Constantine brought his army <u>south</u> and took the top part of Northumbria away from the Vikings. He handed it to an English earl, but Constantine remained as overlord.

A Viking sandwich

Not longer after <u>Constantine</u> began pushing down from <u>Scotland</u> to re-take Scottish lands that had been held by the Vikings, <u>Athelstan</u> was crowned king of the Anglo-Saxons. This picture shows King Athelstan.

Athelstan began <u>moving up England</u> from the south, sweeping the Danes northwards out of the Danelaw.

The Vikings were <u>trapped</u> between Athelstan and Constantine...

How do you think the Vikings felt during this time?

Stalemate in Scotland

By AD 928, Athelstan had retaken <u>York</u> from the Vikings, and brought it back under <u>English rule</u>.

In AD 934 he marched north, determined to take over Scotland. His idea was to <u>unite all of Britain</u>. He attacked Constantine at the fortress of <u>Dunnottar</u>, but was <u>unable to defeat him</u>.

The two kings had reached a stalemate. There was clearly enough power on Athelstan's side to make Constantine back down, but not enough for Athelstan to claim a complete victory. The two sides parted, and the stage was set for a <u>rematch</u>...

Athelstan vs Constantine – the rematch

In 937, at <u>Brunanburh</u>, the armies met again. Each king had gathered his allies. It was one of the biggest battles of the time.

What do you think is going on in this picture?

This picture shows what the battle of Brunanburh might have looked like.

Athelstan and Constantine's armies fought each other but <u>Athelstan won</u>.

<u>Athelstan</u> had secured his country's northern borders and retook a lot of the land that had been controlled by the Vikings. Athelstan is considered to be the first <u>King of England</u>. <u>Constantine</u> remained <u>King of Scotland</u>.

It's one battle after another...

Britain was very unstable and rarely peaceful — people were always fighting for control. During Athelstan and Constantine's battles, the Vikings were trapped in the middle.

Vikings in the 10th Century

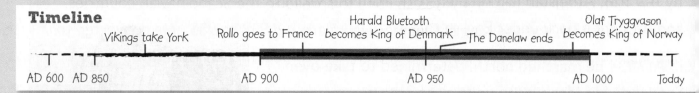

Timeline

Vikings take York — Rollo goes to France — Harald Bluetooth becomes King of Denmark — The Danelaw ends — Olaf Tryggvason becomes King of Norway

AD 600 AD 850   AD 900   AD 950   AD 1000   Today

In AD 954, the <u>last remaining Viking king</u> in England was defeated. The Danelaw was <u>over</u>.
Any Danes left behind were ruled by an <u>English king</u>.

What do you think life was like for the Vikings that stayed in England?

Living together in harmony...?

By this point, the Vikings had settled into British society. They had been living with the
Anglo-Saxons in England for at least three generations. They had <u>married</u> Anglo-Saxons
and were <u>farming</u> as the Anglo-Saxons did. They were also eating the same <u>foods</u>, obeying
the same <u>laws</u> and dying of the same <u>diseases</u>.

But what was life like for their Norse relatives back home in Scandinavia? Let's find out...

Claiming new land

The Vikings of Norway, Sweden and Denmark hadn't stopped
travelling overseas. They hadn't stopped <u>raiding</u> either, or trying
to take <u>land</u> away from other countries.

In AD 911, one of these Vikings, <u>Rollo</u>, was living
in France. He tried to raid Paris, but failed.
Later he made a treaty with the French king,
which allowed him to settle in lands in the north
of France.

These lands became the duchy of Normandy.
The Normans who settled in France would later be
part of England's history.

This is a statue of Rollo
which stands in Norway.

Christianity spreads

By the 10th century, Christianity was starting to spread to the Scandinavian countries. Harald Bluetooth was the King of Denmark from around 958 to 985. He converted to Christianity and wanted everyone else in Denmark to become Christian too.

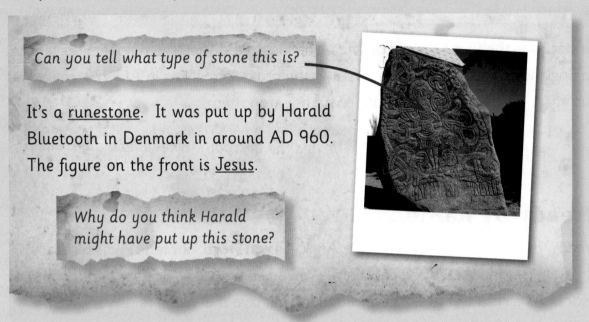

Can you tell what type of stone this is?

It's a runestone. It was put up by Harald Bluetooth in Denmark in around AD 960. The figure on the front is Jesus.

Why do you think Harald might have put up this stone?

Religious pressure

Olaf Tryggvason was a Viking warrior who was involved in raids on Britain. Later, he converted to Christianity and was baptised in England. In AD 995, he became King of Norway.

Olaf is thought to have built the first Christian church in Norway. He also wanted the people living under his rule to convert to Christianity. However, not everyone wanted to give up their Pagan religion, so he began to convert people to Christianity by force.

This is a statue of Olaf Tryggvason that now stands in Norway.

How do you think the people living in Norway at the time felt about Olaf?

Why do you think there's a statue of Olaf in Norway today?

Just when it looked like it was all settling down...

It's good to know that the Vikings of Scandinavia hadn't stopped being Vikings — they were still sailing the seas, raiding, invading and generally causing mayhem! They were starting to convert to Christianity though — either willingly or by force.

Aethelred is Unready!

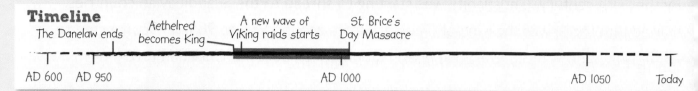

Timeline

The Danelaw ends · Aethelred becomes King · A new wave of Viking raids starts · St. Brice's Day Massacre

AD 600   AD 950   AD 1000   AD 1050   Today

Athelstan was the first King of England. The kings who took the throne after him tried to keep England peaceful. However, after <u>Aethelred</u> became king in AD 978, the Viking raids begun again on a large scale, and he could not stop them.

King Aethelred is known as 'Aethelred the Unready'. Why do you think this is?

Unready by name...

'Unready' is a rough translation of the Anglo-Saxon word 'unraede', which means '<u>bad advice</u>' — and Aethelred certainly received some bad advice from his council of advisors. As a result of this, Aethelred didn't manage the Viking raids very well.

The Danish are back... groan

The first of the new wave of Viking raids began in AD 980, when small parties of raiders began to try the defences of the ports along the <u>south coast</u> of England. It became clear to them that the king <u>didn't</u> have the <u>power</u> or <u>organisation</u> to defend the country from these raids, and so more and more Vikings came.

This picture shows what the coast might have looked like during a Viking raid.

Can you see anything that shows it's a raid?

Paying the price

Aethelred eventually gave in, and <u>paid</u> the Vikings to go away. This was known as paying Danegeld.

Paying Danegeld was not a new thing (even Alfred the Great had to do it), but the amount paid was <u>enormous</u>. Aethelred paid 3300 kg of silver, which would be worth over a million pounds at today's prices! His council hoped that the Vikings would go away for good once they'd been paid.

They didn't. In AD 994, Aethelred paid Olaf Tryggvason to stop him raiding London, and in AD 1002 he paid the Danish army.

Why do you think Aethelred kept paying the Vikings when it didn't work the first time?

What do you think Aethelred should have done instead?

A terrible revenge

In November 1002, Aethelred ordered that all <u>Danish men</u> in Britain should be <u>killed</u>. It became known as the <u>St Brice's Day</u> massacre, and archaeological evidence suggests that hundreds of male Danes were killed. <u>Mass graves</u> containing the skeletons of young males have been found, which have been linked by archaeologists to this massacre.

By Danish men, Aethelred meant anyone of Viking descent.

Why do you think Aethelred made this order?

Everyone had to contribute to paying the Danegeld, so Aethelred's people would have been <u>angry</u>. Aethelred may have also feared that he'd never get rid of the Vikings without drastic action. Whatever reasons he had, killing so many people was an extreme step.

England paid a huge amount of money to the Vikings

Aethered took extreme measures to deal with the Vikings. It seems like he was getting so worried that the Danes were going to break their Danegeld deal and take over England again, that he went as far as calling a massacre. Grim stuff. I sense Viking revenge...

King Canute and Emma

In Norway, news of the St Brice's Day Massacre was received with <u>shock</u> and <u>anger</u>.

What do you think happened next?

Anglo-Saxons

<u>1002</u>: King Aethelred ordered the <u>St-Brice's Day massacre</u>.

Between <u>1002</u>, and <u>1013</u>, England fought against, and bought off the Danes, raising more than 38 000 kg of silver to do so. This made England extremely <u>poor</u>. By <u>1013</u>, England was exhausted. <u>Aethelred fled</u> to Normandy.

<u>Aethelred</u> returned to England and <u>fought Canute</u> for the throne.

<u>1016</u>: <u>Aethelred died</u>. The crown passed to his son <u>Edmund Ironside</u> who continued to fight Canute. Only 6 months later <u>Edmund died</u>. He may have been <u>murdered</u>.

Vikings

King Sweyn Forkbeard of Norway was Harald Bluetooth's son. It is said that his sister died in the attacks. He <u>invaded England</u> in <u>1003</u>.

<u>Sweyn</u> became King of England... but <u>died</u> a few weeks later. Did the crown pass to <u>Sweyn's son</u>, <u>Canute</u>?

<u>Canute</u> became <u>King of England</u>.

Could a Danish king govern England?

Canute governed England well. He <u>stopped</u> the Vikings <u>raiding</u> — because many of the people who had been raiding were his men! He also used the English people and his own Danish Vikings to <u>conquer</u> most of <u>Scandinavia</u>. He made sure that Britain was involved in international <u>trade</u>.

To many English people, Canute would always be a Viking raider. What else do you think Canute could have done to get the English to accept him as king?

Emma of Normandy...

Emma was the Duke of Normandy's daughter and Aethelred's <u>second wife</u>. They had three children: Edward (who later became King Edward the Confessor), Alfred and Goda.

...and of England... and Denmark

When Aethelred <u>died</u> in 1016, it was <u>Edmund Ironside</u>, Aethelred's son from his first marriage, who became king.

However, when he died as well, Emma managed to <u>defend</u> London against the threat of Canute. A huge change in the politics of the time then happened. A <u>marriage</u> was arranged between Canute and... Emma! So it was Emma who helped the English to <u>accept Canute</u>.

This daughter of a Duke of Normandy, who had become an <u>Anglo-Saxon</u> Queen of England, was now a <u>Viking</u> Queen of England and Denmark.

Why do you think the English were more accepting of Canute once he'd married Emma?

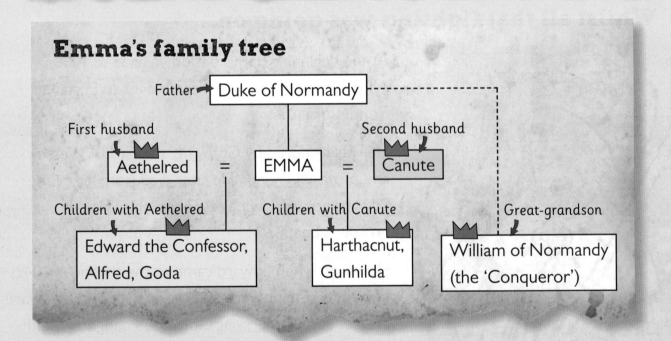

Emma's family tree

Father → Duke of Normandy

First husband — Aethelred = EMMA = Canute — Second husband

Children with Aethelred: Edward the Confessor, Alfred, Goda

Children with Canute: Harthacnut, Gunhilda

Great-grandson: William of Normandy (the 'Conqueror')

Canute eventually ruled England

The St Brice's Day massacre eventually resulted in Viking rule in England once more. Understandably, the Vikings were pretty upset with what King Aethelred had ordered, and so they came back to invade. Eventually, they had hold of England again.

The Kings After Canute

Timeline

Canute becomes
King of England

Canute dies

Edward becomes
King of England

AD 600   AD 1000   AD 1050   AD 1100   Today

When Canute died, there were four options for the throne of England. Two options were <u>Edward</u> and <u>Alfred</u>, Queen Emma's sons by Aethelred. The others were <u>Harold Harefoot</u>, Canute's son by his first wife, and <u>Harthacnut</u>, Emma and Canute's son.

What do you think happened?

Who do you think should have got the throne?

King confusion

<u>Harthacnut</u> was acting as king in Denmark after his father, Canute, died. He should have become King of England too, but had to stay in Denmark to fight for his throne there.

<u>Harold</u> looked after the throne whilst Harthacnut was away, but he took it for <u>himself</u> in 1037. <u>Harthacnut</u> re-took his throne in 1040. On his death in 1042, It passed to <u>Edward</u>.

Whilst all that fighting was going on...

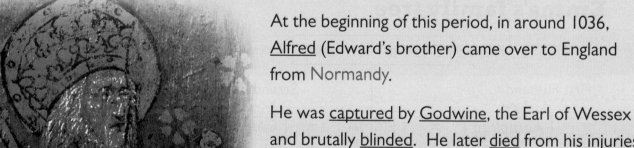

At the beginning of this period, in around 1036, <u>Alfred</u> (Edward's brother) came over to England from Normandy.

He was <u>captured</u> by <u>Godwine</u>, the Earl of Wessex and brutally <u>blinded</u>. He later <u>died</u> from his injuries. Edward held Godwine responsible for his brother's death.

However, when <u>Edward</u> came to the throne in 1042, he needed the powerful Godwine's <u>support</u>. Edward even ended up <u>marrying</u> Godwine's daughter, Edith.

How do you think Edward felt about this?

← This is a painting of King Edward.

Godwine just won't go away

The English king needed the support of powerful land-owners and earls, and couldn't govern without it.

In 1051, Edward managed to exile Godwine and his sons after an argument, but he ended up having to allow them back when they arrived with an army a year later. Other important earls wouldn't support Edward against their friend.

It was impossible for kings to rule without the support of their earls. The way society worked meant that if the king needed an army to fight an invader, he had to rely on his earls to raise the 'fyrd' — the armed men they collected from their own estates. Although English society had moved from several kings to one king, the earls still held great power.

This is part of a famous tapestry, showing King Edward.

What do you think is happening in this scene?

What about the ordinary people?

It's important to remember that whether they were being ruled by Romans, Anglo-Saxons or Vikings, ordinary people in England spent their lives making sure they had enough to eat, being with their families, and trying not to be killed in battle. They had little say in who would become the next king or queen.

Do you think that this was fair? Why, or why not?

It wasn't easy being king...

King Edward believed that one of his earls, Godwine, was responsible for the death of his brother. However, he still had to accept Godwine's support and even marry into his family. Being a successful king relied on having plenty of support — it wasn't an easy job.

The Conqueror is Coming

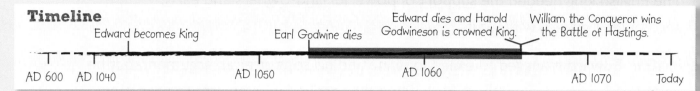

Timeline

Edward becomes King — Earl Godwine dies — Edward dies and Harold Godwineson is crowned King. — William the Conqueror wins the Battle of Hastings.

AD 600 AD 1040   AD 1050   AD 1060   AD 1070   Today

Earl Godwine died in 1053, but by 1057, several of his sons held powerful positions. One of them, Harold Godwineson was Earl of Wessex. Another was Earl of Northumbria. King Edward was surrounded by powerful men — and could not fight them!

How do you think this made King Edward feel? Why?

Confessions of a saint

Edward is known as 'Edward the Confessor'. He lived a very religious life, giving money to the church, supporting Christian monks, going to church regularly and following all the church rules. He seemed a good king, and England was generally peaceful and safe under his rule. After his death he was made a saint.

King Edward's seal

Noticeably Norman?

Edward had spent most of his childhood in Normandy in France. Because of this he was Norman in attitude, speech, and belief.

Edward employed some of his Norman friends at court, which didn't go down well with some of the English earls.

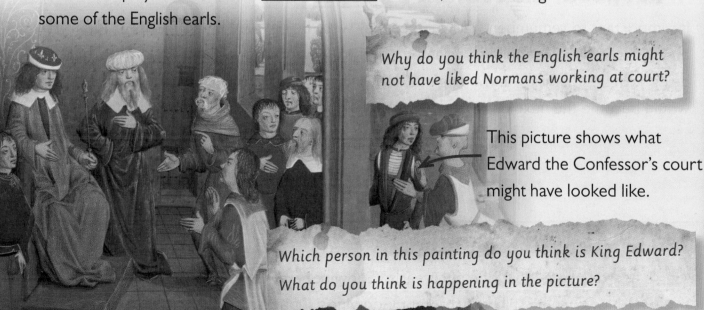

Why do you think the English earls might not have liked Normans working at court?

This picture shows what Edward the Confessor's court might have looked like.

Which person in this painting do you think is King Edward? What do you think is happening in the picture?

A crown but no king...

Edward didn't have any children, so there was no one to take over the throne when Edward died in 1066. Several people wanted it though...

1. Harold Godwineson claimed Edward had offered him the throne on his death bed.
2. William, the Duke of Normandy, claimed Edward had promised him the crown in 1051.
3. Harald Hardrada, the King of Norway, also thought he had a right to be king.

> Who do you think the people of England wanted as king? Do you think they cared?

The decision sparks anger

On Edward's death, it was Harold Godwineson who was crowned King of England. William was outraged and began building ships to invade England. Harald Hardrada also decided to invade and headed from Norway to Northumbria.

When Harald Hardrada invaded, the new King Harold marched north to meet him with an army. They fought at Stamford Bridge, and Harald Hardrada was killed. One opponent was out of the way!

Because King Harold had marched north to meet Hardrada's invasion, he wasn't ready for the invasion of Normans that happened straight after. King Harold had to quickly march his army back down south.

On October 14th 1066, William, Duke of Normandy, defeated and killed Harold at the Battle of Hastings. He became known as William the Conqueror and England became Norman. The last successful invasion of England had just changed its history for ever...

This is part of the famous Bayeux Tapestry. It shows William's troops preparing themselves for the Battle of Hastings.

It's battle after battle for the kings of England...

As soon as Harold took the title of King of England, he had to start defending that right. Other people wanted the throne, and they were prepared to come and fight for it. In the end, it was the Normans that won the day and seized the throne.

Glossary

Term	Definition
afterlife	Where some people believe you go after death.
ally	A person, group or country who is working with you for a particular purpose.
amber	A hard yellow or orange substance that can be used in jewellery.
Anglo-Saxons	The main group of people living in Britain when the Vikings invaded.
archaeological evidence	Objects that get dug up by archaeologists, which we can use to find out what life was like in the past. For example, coins, pottery, bones, etc.
archaeologist	A person who studies history by digging up objects and using them to tell us about the past.
baptise	To accept someone into the Christian religion.
blood-feud	A violent argument between families that takes place over many years.
Christian	A person who follows the religion based on the teachings of Jesus Christ.
Danegeld	Money paid to the Vikings to stop them from raiding.
Danelaw	The area of land in Britain that the Danish Vikings ruled over.
Danes	People from Denmark. In the past, people in Britain sometimes referred to all Vikings as Danes.
duchy	An area within a country, which is ruled by a duke.
estate	The land owned by a lord.
excavation	The process whereby archaeologists dig in the ground to find objects and buildings from the past.
exile	To send someone out of a country and ban them from coming back.
famine	A serious shortage of food over a wide area of land.

fortify	Build <u>defences</u> to <u>protect</u> a place or building from attack.
fyrd	An Anglo-Saxon <u>army</u>.
harvest	The time of year when the <u>crops</u> are cut down to provide <u>food</u>.
hilt	The <u>handle</u> of a sword.
hoard	A <u>store</u> of <u>money</u> or <u>treasure</u>.
international	Involving more than one <u>country</u>.
ivory	The hard, white substance that animal <u>tusks</u> are made from.
justice system	A system for making sure that people <u>don't break the law</u>, and for <u>punishing</u> them for their <u>crimes</u>.
knarr	A <u>Viking ship</u> used for <u>long voyages</u> and <u>trading</u> because it had lots of storage <u>space</u> for transporting supplies.
longship	A <u>Viking ship</u> used for <u>fighting</u> and carrying out <u>raids</u>.
legend	A <u>story</u> set in human <u>history</u>, which historians haven't been able to prove actually happened.
loot	<u>Stolen money</u> or <u>treasure</u>.
massacre	The <u>murder</u> of a large number of people.
mead	An <u>alcoholic drink</u> made from <u>honey</u>.
monastery	A place where people who have dedicated their lives to <u>religion</u>, such as <u>monks</u> or <u>nuns</u>, live.
navigate	Find the <u>right way</u> to where you're going, across the land or the sea.
Normans	People who came from Scandinavia and <u>settled</u> in <u>northern France</u>, in an area now called <u>Normandy</u>, in the 10th century.

Norsemen	The name given to <u>people</u> living in <u>Scandinavia</u> at the time of the <u>Vikings</u>. It means '<u>men of the North</u>'.
outlawing	Stripping someone of all their legal rights, so that they're <u>not protected</u> by the law. For example, somebody could hurt them but not be punished for it.
overlord	A lord who is in <u>overall charge </u> of an area of land, including all the <u>other lords</u> in the area.
Pagan religion	A group of traditional religions. Many of these religions worship several <u>gods</u> or <u>goddesses</u>, and <u>nature</u> is seen as very important.
plunder	Take <u>loot</u> during a raid, often causing damage at the same time.
priory	A <u>small monastery</u> (place where monks or nuns live).
raid	A <u>surprise attack</u>.
rune	A <u>letter</u> from the alphabet used by the Vikings.
runestone	A <u>standing stone</u> engraved with <u>writing</u> and sometimes a <u>picture</u>.
saga	A long Viking <u>poem</u>, which tells stories of <u>warriors</u> and <u>heros</u>.
Scandinavia	The countries of <u>Norway</u>, <u>Sweden</u> and <u>Denmark</u>. This is the area the Vikings came from.
stalemate	When two sides are fighting, but <u>neither</u> is able to <u>win</u>.
trade	<u>Sell</u> items for money, or <u>swap</u> them for other items.
treaty	An <u>agreement</u> made between two or more people, groups or countries.
Valhalla	The place Vikings believed they would go <u>after death</u>, if they died <u>fighting bravely</u> in <u>battle</u>.
wergild	The <u>money</u> a <u>person</u> or piece of <u>property</u> was thought to be worth. If a person was <u>killed</u>, their family would be paid wergild by the <u>killer</u>.

What did the monks think?

It was recorded in the Anglo-Saxon Chronicle that <u>bad omens</u> were seen before the Vikings arrived.

Great <u>lightning storms</u>, 'whirlwinds', and 'fiery dragons' in the sky were some of the things mentioned, as well as a <u>great</u> famine. Some Christians believed these had been a <u>warning</u> of the invasion, and that the Viking raids were a result of people living <u>sinful lives</u>.

> The Anglo-Saxon Chronicle is a history of Anglo-Saxon Britain. It was written between the late 8th and early 12th centuries.

So what happened after the Lindisfarne raid?

The Vikings who raided Lindisfarne would have seen that the small church communities along the shores of Britain were <u>easy targets</u>. They were all in <u>isolated</u> places, far from help.

The raid on Lindisfarne terrified the church. The Vikings didn't just <u>steal</u> things and ruin the priory — they also took some monks as <u>slaves</u> and <u>killed</u> others. This painting shows what an artist thinks the raid on Lindisfarne might have looked like.

The Vikings had not finished with Britain after that one raid.

They continued to raid <u>monasteries</u> on the British coast. The monks eventually <u>abandoned Lindisfarne</u>.

> How do you think the monks felt when they finally left Lindisfarne?
>
> Why do you think they might have felt this way?

Churches were treasure troves for the Vikings

The Vikings' first raid in England targeted the priory on Lindisfarne Island. It wasn't defended and so the Vikings were easily able to take what they wanted. It would have been a worrying time — watching out for more Vikings arriving in their longships.

Violent Vikings?

Timeline

		Vikings raid Lindisfarne		Vikings settle in Iceland	Government set up at Thingvellir			
AD 600	AD 750	AD 800	AD 850	AD 900	AD 950	AD 1000	Today

Vikings are thought of as being pretty <u>violent</u>. Historians <u>question</u> whether they were really like this, and whether they deserve to be thought of as the criminals of Europe.

Using what you've leant about the Vikings so far, what do you think?

Exaggerated tales?

Many written sources from the time describe the Vikings as violent. However, some of these sources were written a <u>long way</u> from the action. For example, a man called Alcuin wrote a description of the raid on Lindisfarne when he was working in France. His writing may have been <u>exaggerated</u> because he was horrified that anyone would attack the Christian church.

Stories from the sagas

The Norse sagas are long poems that tell <u>stories</u> about <u>Norsemen</u> and <u>Vikings</u>. They were written in the <u>Old Norse</u> language in about the 13th century. The sagas include descriptions of the <u>violence</u> in Viking society. For example, this story is part of Njal's Saga:

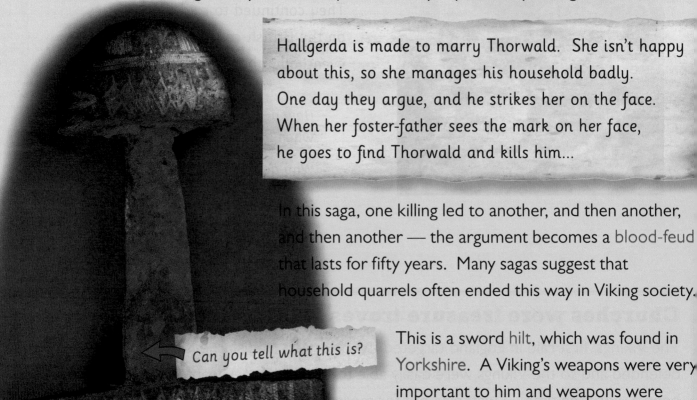

Hallgerda is made to marry Thorwald. She isn't happy about this, so she manages his household badly.
One day they argue, and he strikes her on the face.
When her foster-father sees the mark on her face,
he goes to find Thorwald and kills him...

In this saga, one killing led to another, and then another, and then another — the argument becomes a blood-feud that lasts for fifty years. Many sagas suggest that household quarrels often ended this way in Viking society.

Can you tell what this is?

This is a sword hilt, which was found in Yorkshire. A Viking's weapons were very important to him and weapons were mentioned in several sagas.

Crime didn't go unpunished...

The Vikings might have been violent, but they weren't completely lawless. The Vikings had a justice system, which developed as time went on. It relied on <u>fines</u>, wergild, or outlawing to punish crime.

If a person was killed, their family would be paid <u>wergild</u> by the killer in compensation.

Time to step up and be judged

Some Vikings moved to Iceland in around AD 870. In AD 930, at a place in Iceland called 'Thingvellir', the Vikings set up a government (which they called <u>Althing</u>).

Vikings would meet at Thingvellir to <u>settle quarrels</u> and <u>judge crimes</u>. Viking laws were originally not written down, but were kept by a '<u>law-speaker</u>' — an experienced man who knew all of the laws, and could remember what penalties were appropriate for different crimes.

The law-speaker stood on 'Law Rock' to speak.

Do you think having a law-speaker was a good idea? Can you think of anyone with a job like that of a law-speaker today?

Eyeing up the evidence

The evidence shows that early Viking society was <u>violent</u>, and the <u>blood-feud</u> was the way of settling quarrels. Over a few centuries, Viking society became more <u>civilised</u> — a system of laws and rules was developed.

However, it's important to remember that because they believed in courage and honour the Vikings <u>didn't fear</u> death in battle. Brave men were made into heroes, so they could afford to be ruthless and deadly when raiding — they had a <u>different view</u> on violence to us.

What do you think now that you know a bit more? Did the Vikings deserve their reputation?

Everybody's got an opinion...

Always look at where historical evidence has come from. Was it written at the <u>time</u>, or in the <u>same place</u> as the events happening? And <u>who</u> wrote it? With history, you have to always <u>question</u> the evidence — you can't just trust everything you read straight away.

More Viking Visits

Timeline

| | | Vikings raid Lindisfarne | Vikings settle on Orkney | | Vikings attack the Isle of Sheppey | | |

AD 600   AD 750   AD 800   AD 850   Today

After their first raid on Lindisfarne, the Vikings continued to attack the British coast.

This painting shows what an artist thinks it might have been like for the people of Tynemouth, when they saw the Viking ships approaching.

What are the people in this picture doing?

How do you think the people of Tynemouth felt when they saw Viking ships in the distance?

Orkney – a great place to stay

One of the first places that the Vikings lived in Britain was Orkney — a group of islands at the very top of Scotland.

Orkney was only one or two days sail away from the Norwegian coast, and there was free land. So it was the perfect place for the Norsemen to settle with their families. It also proved to be an ideal base from which to raid the rest of Britain.

The picture below shows the remains of a Viking settlement on Orkney.

Vikings in England

The Vikings who had plundered Lindisfarne appear to have been from <u>Norway</u>, possibly based in Orkney. The Vikings then spent the next thirty years or so making regular attacks on the <u>Scottish</u> and <u>Irish coasts</u>, rather than England, although there were also some raids against English monasteries in the <u>north</u>.

The next major raid against England was from the Danish Vikings, who attacked the Isle of Sheppey in <u>Kent</u>, in AD 835.

For thirty years after that, Vikings regularly attacked the English coasts. This painting is of the English waiting for Viking ships to arrive. It was painted in 1890 — about 1000 years after the Viking raids took place.

What do you think the artist based his picture on? Do you think this picture shows a scene that really happened at the time? Why or why not?

Vikings – foe... or friend?

Not everybody on the coast of Britain lived in fear of the Vikings.

The people of Cornwall, for example, teamed up with Vikings on more than one occasion to fight the Anglo-Saxons in other parts of Britain.

Tin has been mined in Cornwall for over 4000 years.

Does this give you a clue as to one reason why the Vikings might have been friendly with the people of Cornwall?

The Cornish people may have traded with the Vikings.
Cornwall was a popular trading partner because it always had tin to trade.

They did like to be beside the seaside...

The Vikings came in ships across the sea from Scandinavia, so most of their raids took place on coastal areas and they didn't tend to venture very far inland at first. The people in these coastal areas often lived in fear of the Vikings returning year after year.

Viking Victories

Timeline

Vikings attack the Isle of Sheppey   Vikings attack London   The Great Heathen Army attacks Britain

AD 600   AD 800   AD 850   AD 900   Today

Between AD 833 and AD 851, the Vikings <u>repeatedly attacked</u> the English coast.
Each time they landed, they were eventually <u>beaten back</u> by an army of Anglo-Saxons.

The Angles and Saxons had once invaded Britain themselves. How do you think they felt about the Viking invaders?

The tide starts to turn

In AD 850, 350 Viking ships entered the Thames and stormed London and Canterbury.
The Anglo-Saxons kept control of the cities, but they couldn't drive the Vikings away.
The Vikings spent the winter in England — it was clear they were <u>growing stronger</u>.

The king with the hairy trousers

Around this point in Viking history, historians come across a figure called 'Ragnar Lodbrok', which loosely translates as 'Ragnar Hairy-Trousers'.

Nobody knows for sure whether Ragnar <u>really existed</u>. Someone like him did — a powerful leader who destroyed Paris, raided England, and generally behaved in true Viking style!

According to legend, his death at the hands of an Anglo-Saxon king inspired the Great Heathen Army's attack on Britain in <u>AD 865</u>.

This picture shows what an artist thinks Ragnar might have looked like.

How is Ragnar made to look like a leader in this picture?

Enter the Great Heathen Army

The Great Heathen Army really did exist. It was a large group of Vikings, who set up camp in East Anglia. The locals there gave them <u>horses</u> in exchange for <u>peace</u>.

The army spent the winter in East Anglia before moving on to <u>raid</u> the <u>north of England</u>.

Caught off guard

At this time, England was split into different <u>kingdoms</u>, each ruled over by a <u>different</u> Anglo-Saxon king. This map shows the Anglo-Saxon kingdoms in AD 865.

The kingdoms all fought amongst themselves and <u>weren't</u> <u>organised</u> enough to fight the Vikings and drive them away.

When the Vikings began to turn up in <u>huge numbers</u>, the Saxons just <u>couldn't</u> compete.

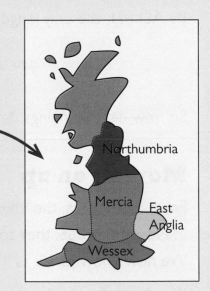

Fickle Fyrds

A fyrd was the name for an Anglo-Saxon army. Fyrds were only called together in times of trouble. They assembled for a <u>short time</u> at the request of a lord (or 'thegn') and the men who fought in them were expected to provide their <u>own food</u> and <u>weapons</u>.

Why do you think the system of fyrds made it difficult to fight Viking invaders like the Great Heathen Army?

Having fyrds instead of a large permanent army meant it was difficult to quickly assemble enough men to fight off large numbers of Vikings.

Vikings One, Anglo-Saxons Nil...

Ragnar Lodbrok might not have existed, but the Vikings did have strong leaders who lead them to victory against the Anglo-Saxons. The Vikings eventually conquered part of England, but it took them a while and it wasn't all plain sailing, as we're about to see...

Defeating the Anglo-Saxons

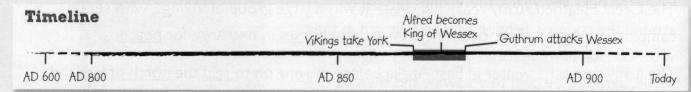

Timeline

Vikings take York — Alfred becomes King of Wessex — Guthrum attacks Wessex

AD 600 AD 800 — AD 850 — AD 900 — Today

Over the next few years the Vikings defeated each Anglo-Saxon kingdom, one by one. By AD 871, the only kingdom left to resist the Vikings was Wessex.

How do you think it felt to be an ordinary Anglo-Saxon at this time?

So how did the Vikings defeat the Anglo-Saxons? Let's find out...

Moving on up

From East Anglia, the Vikings moved up through the <u>north</u> and <u>east</u> of England. In November 866, they took the Anglo-Saxon city of Eoforwic, which they renamed <u>Jorvik</u>. We now know Jorvik as York.

The Anglo-Saxons later tried to re-take the city, but they were unsuccessful and the <u>Northumbrian Kings</u> Aelle and Osbert were <u>killed</u>.

Edmund the unfortunate

In AD 870, the Vikings returned to East Anglia, where the people had tried to buy their friendship with horses.

According to one written record, the Vikings killed the East Anglian king, <u>Edmund</u>, in battle. However, <u>Christian monks</u> later said that he was whipped, tied to a tree and shot with arrows because he would not stop being a Christian. He was later made a <u>saint</u>.

As with most stories of this kind, we can't tell whether this <u>really happened</u> or is a legend.

What do you think really happened to Edmund?

Why do you think the monks might have told a different story to other written records?